MAD LIBS

DANCE MANIA
MAD LIBS

By Roger Price and Leonard Stern

Mad Libs
An Imprint of Penguin Random House

MAD LIBS
Penguin Young Readers Group
An Imprint of Penguin Random House LLC

Mad Libs format and text copyright © 2009 by Penguin Random House LLC.
All rights reserved.

Concept created by Roger Price & Leonard Stern

Published by Mad Libs,
an imprint of Penguin Random House LLC,
345 Hudson Street, New York, New York 10014.
Printed in the USA.

Penguin supports copyright. Copyright fuels creativity, encourages diverse voices,
promotes free speech, and creates a vibrant culture. Thank you for buying an authorized
edition of this book and for complying with copyright laws by not reproducing, scanning,
or distributing any part of it in any form without permission. You are supporting writers
and allowing Penguin to continue to publish books for every reader.

ISBN 9780843137125
25

MAD LIBS is a registered trademark of Penguin Random House LLC.

MAD LIBS® is a game for people who don't like games!
It can be played by one, two, three, four, or forty.

• RIDICULOUSLY SIMPLE DIRECTIONS

In this tablet you will find stories containing blank spaces where words
are left out. One player, the READER, selects one of these stories. The
READER does not tell anyone what the story is about. Instead, he/she asks
the other players, the WRITERS, to give him/her words. These words are
used to fill in the blank spaces in the story.

• TO PLAY

The READER asks each WRITER in turn to call out a word—an adjective or
a noun or whatever the space calls for—and uses them to fill in the blank
spaces in the story. The result is a MAD LIBS® game.

When the READER then reads the completed MAD LIBS® game to the other
players, they will discover that they have written a story that is fantastic,
screamingly funny, shocking, silly, crazy, or just plain dumb—depending
upon which words each WRITER called out.

• EXAMPLE (*Before* and *After*)

" _____ !" he said _____
            EXCLAMATION   ADVERB

as he jumped into his convertible _____ and
                                          NOUN

drove off with his _____ wife.
                          ADJECTIVE

" _____*Ouch*_____ !" he said _____*Stupidly*_____
            EXCLAMATION   ADVERB

as he jumped into his convertible _____*Cat*_____ and
                                          NOUN

drove off with his _____*brave*_____ wife.
                          ADJECTIVE

In case you have forgotten what adjectives, adverbs, nouns, and verbs are, here is a quick review:

An ADJECTIVE describes something or somebody. *Lumpy*, *soft*, *ugly*, *messy*, and *short* are adjectives.

An ADVERB tells how something is done. It modifies a verb and usually ends in "ly." *Modestly*, *stupidly*, *greedily*, and *carefully* are adverbs.

A NOUN is the name of a person, place, or thing. *Sidewalk*, *umbrella*, *bridle*, *bathtub*, and *nose* are nouns.

A VERB is an action word. *Run*, *pitch*, *jump*, and *swim* are verbs. Put the verbs in past tense if the directions say PAST TENSE. *Ran*, *pitched*, *jumped*, and *swam* are verbs in the past tense.

When we ask for A PLACE, we mean any sort of place: a country or city (*Spain*, *Cleveland*) or a room (*bathroom*, *kitchen*).

An EXCLAMATION or SILLY WORD is any sort of funny sound, gasp, grunt, or outcry, like *Wow!*, *Ouch!*, *Whomp!*, *Ick!*, and *Gadzooks!*

When we ask for specific words, like a NUMBER, a COLOR, an ANIMAL, or a PART OF THE BODY, we mean a word that is one of those things, like *seven*, *blue*, *horse*, or *head*.

When we ask for a PLURAL, it means more than one. For example, *cat* pluralized is *cats*.

MAD LIBS® is fun to play with friends, but you can also play it by yourself! To begin with, DO NOT look at the story on the page below. Fill in the blanks on this page with the words called for. Then, using the words you have selected, fill in the blank spaces in the story.

Now you've created your own hilarious MAD LIBS® game!

THE LATEST DANCE CRAZE

ADJECTIVE _____

A PLACE _____

PERSON IN ROOM _____

VERB ENDING IN "ING" _____

NOUN _____

ADJECTIVE _____

PART OF THE BODY (PLURAL) _____

PART OF THE BODY _____

ADJECTIVE _____

NUMBER _____

ADJECTIVE _____

ADVERB _____

NUMBER _____

ADJECTIVE _____

PART OF THE BODY _____

PLURAL NOUN _____

PART OF THE BODY _____

ADVERB _____

ADJECTIVE _____

MAD LBS

I DREAM OF DANCING

You've always dreamed of growing up to be a/an _____
                                                ADJECTIVE

professional dancer, with audiences giving you _____
                                          VERB ENDING IN "ING"

ovations and showering the stage with _____. Which
                                         PLURAL NOUN

_____ dancing career will you choose?
   ADJECTIVE

1. A prima _____ for a/an _____ ballet company.
              NOUN   ADJECTIVE

   You'll leap, twirl, and _____ across the stage in a/an
                              VERB

   _____ tutu.
      ADJECTIVE

2. A famous _____-ette who dances at _____
                 NOUN   NOUN

   City Music Hall. Your _____ high kicks will be
                            ADJECTIVE

   known throughout (the) _____!
                            A PLACE

3. A competitive ballroom _____. You'll glide along
                             NOUN

   wearing a floor-length _____ while your partner
                             NOUN

   carries a long-stemmed _____ in his mouth.
                             NOUN

From DANCE MANIA MAD LIBS® • Copyright © 2009 by Penguin Random House LLC.

MAD LIBS® is fun to play with friends, but you can also play it by yourself! To begin with, DO NOT look at the story on the page below. Fill in the blanks on this page with the words called for. Then, using the words you have selected, fill in the blank spaces in the story.

Now you've created your own hilarious MAD LIBS® game!

HEY THERE, COVER GIRL

PERSON IN ROOM _____

ADJECTIVE _____

ADJECTIVE _____

ANIMAL _____

PLURAL NOUN _____

NOUN _____

PLURAL NOUN _____

ADJECTIVE _____

PART OF THE BODY _____

ADJECTIVE _____

PART OF THE BODY (PLURAL) _____

NOUN _____

ADVERB _____

ADJECTIVE _____

ADJECTIVE _____

NOUN _____

PART OF THE BODY (PLURAL) _____

ADJECTIVE _____

MAD LIBS

HEY THERE, COVER GIRL

Greetings, _____.com fans! Today I'm going to blog about
PERSON IN ROOM

my photo shoot for _____ *Girl* magazine. When I got to
ADJECTIVE

the _____ set, they immediately sent me to wardrobe,
ADJECTIVE

where the stylist outfitted me in a/an _____-print
ANIMAL

dress, a pair of high-heeled _____, and gorgeous
PLURAL NOUN

_____-shaped earrings. Next, the hairdresser
NOUN

put hot _____ in my hair to make it look full and
PLURAL NOUN

_____. The makeup artist then put blush on my
ADJECTIVE

_____ and chose a/an _____ lipstick to
PART OF THE BODY   ADJECTIVE

bring out the color of my _____. I felt prettier
PART OF THE BODY (PLURAL)

than a/an _____ as I posed _____ for the
NOUN   ADVERB

photographer. At the end of the shoot, they told me I had done a

really _____ job—and that I'd definitely be on the cover
ADJECTIVE

of the _____ magazine! So, _____ fans, keep
ADJECTIVE   NOUN

your _____ peeled for my _____ face
PART OF THE BODY (PLURAL)   ADJECTIVE

at a newsstand near you!

From DANCE MANIA MAD LIBS® • Copyright © 2009 by Penguin Random House LLC.

MAD LIBS® is fun to play with friends, but you can also play it by yourself! To begin with, DO NOT look at the story on the page below. Fill in the blanks on this page with the words called for. Then, using the words you have selected, fill in the blank spaces in the story.

Now you've created your own hilarious MAD LIBS® game!

ULTIMATE DANCE PARTY

PERSON IN ROOM _____

SILLY WORD _____

ADJECTIVE _____

ADJECTIVE _____

PERSON IN ROOM _____

ADJECTIVE _____

NOUN _____

ADJECTIVE _____

ADJECTIVE _____

PLURAL NOUN _____

ADJECTIVE _____

NOUN _____

PERSON IN ROOM (MALE) _____

NOUN _____

VERB _____

A PLACE _____

ADJECTIVE _____

MAD LIBS

ULTIMATE DANCE PARTY

To: _____ @ _____ .com
     PERSON IN ROOM   SILLY WORD

Re: Five _____ reasons you should come to my
          ADJECTIVE

_____ dance party
  ADJECTIVE

5. DJ Jammin' _____ will be spinning _____
      PERSON IN ROOM   ADJECTIVE

   tunes until the wee hours of the _____ .
                        NOUN

4. There will be a newly installed _____ dance floor with an
                      ADJECTIVE

   illuminated disco ball and _____ strobe _____ .
                    ADJECTIVE   PLURAL NOUN

3. You can show off your most _____ dance moves.
                      ADJECTIVE

2. Pizza and _____ -sticks will be served.
          NOUN

1. _____ , the cutest _____ at school,
   PERSON IN ROOM (MALE)   NOUN

   will be there and just might ask you to _____ with him.
                          VERB

I hope to see you Saturday at (the) _____ . Get ready to
                      A PLACE

have the most _____ time of your life!
         ADJECTIVE

From DANCE MANIA MAD LIBS® • Copyright © 2009 by Penguin Random House LLC.

MAD LIBS® is fun to play with friends, but you can also play it by yourself! To begin with, DO NOT look at the story on the page below. Fill in the blanks on this page with the words called for. Then, using the words you have selected, fill in the blank spaces in the story.

Now you've created your own hilarious MAD LIBS® game!

GOT DANCE IN YOUR PANTS?

NOUN _____

PLURAL NOUN _____

ADJECTIVE _____

PLURAL NOUN _____

PLURAL NOUN _____

PERSON IN ROOM (FEMALE) _____

NOUN _____

ADJECTIVE _____

ADVERB _____

VERB _____

ADJECTIVE _____

NUMBER _____

NOUN _____

ADJECTIVE _____

NOUN _____

ADJECTIVE _____

PART OF THE BODY _____

NOUN _____

MAD LIBS®

GOT DANCE IN YOUR PANTS?

If you have been bit by the acting _____ and you're
                                          NOUN

looking for an opportunity to show off your _____,
                                                PLURAL NOUN

_____ Productions—the studio that brought
      ADJECTIVE

you _____: *The Musical*—is holding auditions for
      PLURAL NOUN

singers, dancers, and _____ for the lead roles in
                            PLURAL NOUN

Princess _____ *and Sir Dance-a-lot.* For our
              PERSON IN ROOM (FEMALE)

princess, we're seeking a high-energy _____ with a/an
                                            NOUN

_____ voice, who dances _____. The
      ADJECTIVE   ADVERB

Sir-_____-a-lot role calls for a/an _____
        VERB   ADJECTIVE

dancer with a minimum of _____ years of jazz,
                                NUMBER

tap, or _____ dancing. Auditions will include a/an
              NOUN

_____ solo performance and a ballet duet with a
      ADJECTIVE

dancing _____. If you have what it takes, please try out
              NOUN

for our _____ production. And remember to bring a/an
              ADJECTIVE

_____-shot for the casting _____!
  PART OF THE BODY   NOUN

From DANCE MANIA MAD LIBS® • Copyright © 2009 by Penguin Random House LLC.

MAD LIBS® is fun to play with friends, but you can also play it by yourself! To begin with, DO NOT look at the story on the page below. Fill in the blanks on this page with the words called for. Then, using the words you have selected, fill in the blank spaces in the story.

Now you've created your own hilarious MAD LIBS® game!

SO YOU THINK YOU CAN CHEER?

VERB ENDING IN "ING" _____

ADJECTIVE _____

ADVERB _____

NUMBER _____

NUMBER _____

NOUN _____

PART OF THE BODY (PLURAL) _____

PLURAL NOUN _____

NUMBER _____

PLURAL NOUN _____

PART OF THE BODY (PLURAL) _____

PART OF THE BODY (PLURAL) _____

NUMBER _____

PLURAL NOUN _____

NOUN _____

PLURAL NOUN _____

PLURAL NOUN _____

VERB _____

MAD LIBS®
SO YOU THINK YOU CAN CHEER?

We're happy to report there are openings on the school's

varsity cheer-_____ squad. The coach is looking for
                VERB ENDING IN "ING"

_____ girls who can:
        ADJECTIVE

• _____ perform cheers such as "_____,
        ADVERB   NUMBER

_____, six, eight! Who do we appreciate? Go, _____,
   NUMBER   NOUN

go!" while standing on the _____ of other
                            PART OF THE BODY (PLURAL)

cheer-_____.
        PLURAL NOUN

• Do _____ cartwheels in a row while holding
          NUMBER

pom-_____ in both _____.
        PLURAL NOUN   PART OF THE BODY (PLURAL)

• Keep a smile on their _____ when cheering in
                        PART OF THE BODY (PLURAL)

front of _____ screaming _____.
          NUMBER   PLURAL NOUN

Tryouts will be held in the school _____ on Friday. Please
                                    NOUN

wear tennis _____ and comfortable _____,
            PLURAL NOUN   PLURAL NOUN

and be prepared to _____!
                    VERB

From DANCE MANIA MAD LIBS® • Copyright © 2009 by Penguin Random House LLC.

MAD LIBS® is fun to play with friends, but you can also play it by yourself! To begin with, DO NOT look at the story on the page below. Fill in the blanks on this page with the words called for. Then, using the words you have selected, fill in the blank spaces in the story.

Now you've created your own hilarious MAD LIBS® game!

DANCING PRINCESS

ADJECTIVE _____

PERSON IN ROOM (FEMALE) _____

ADJECTIVE _____

A PLACE _____

ADJECTIVE _____

PLURAL NOUN _____

ANIMAL (PLURAL) _____

PESON IN ROOM (MALE) _____

ADJECTIVE _____

PART OF THE BODY _____

NOUN _____

NOUN _____

ADVERB _____

ADJECTIVE _____

PART OF THE BODY _____

NOUN _____

SILLY WORD _____

ADJECTIVE _____

ADVERB _____

MAD LIBS®
DANCING PRINCESS

There once was a/an _____ maiden named
ADJECTIVE

_____ who lived in a/an _____ forest.
PERSON IN ROOM (FEMALE)   ADJECTIVE

One day, she learned that the prince of (the) _____
A PLACE

was having a fancy ball. So she spun a/an _____
ADJECTIVE

gown out of silken _____, jumped in a carriage drawn
PLURAL NOUN

by four _____, and drove to the palace. When she
ANIMAL (PLURAL)

entered the ballroom, Prince _____ was awed by
PERSON IN ROOM (MALE)

how _____ she looked. He gently took her by the
ADJECTIVE

_____ and asked, "May I have this _____?"
PART OF THE BODY   NOUN

They danced till the _____ struck midnight, when
NOUN

she cried, "I must go!" and she disappeared. The prince searched

_____ throughout the land trying to find his
ADVERB

_____ love. When he finally did, he dropped to one
ADJECTIVE

_____ and asked her to be his _____. She
PART OF THE BODY   NOUN

said "Oh, _____," and the _____ couple
SILLY WORD   ADJECTIVE

lived _____ ever after.
ADVERB

From DANCE MANIA MAD LIBS® • Copyright © 2009 by Penguin Random House LLC.

MAD LIBS® is fun to play with friends, but you can also play it by yourself! To begin with, DO NOT look at the story on the page below. Fill in the blanks on this page with the words called for. Then, using the words you have selected, fill in the blank spaces in the story.

Now you've created your own hilarious MAD LIBS® game!

HAPPY DANCE

PLURAL NOUN _____

PLURAL NOUN _____

VERB ENDING IN "ING" _____

VERB ENDING IN "ING" _____

PLURAL NOUN _____

NOUN _____

ADJECTIVE _____

TYPE OF LIQUID _____

VERB ENDING IN "ING" _____

PLURAL NOUN _____

ADJECTIVE _____

PART OF THE BODY _____

PART OF THE BODY (PLURAL) _____

A PLACE _____

ADJECTIVE _____

MAD☺LIBS®

HAPPY DANCE

Some _____ whistle. Some _____ sing.
     PLURAL NOUN   PLURAL NOUN

But when I'm in a happy mood, my toes start _____,
                                VERB ENDING IN "ING"

my fingers start _____, I feel light on my
             VERB ENDING IN "ING"

_____, and I become a dancing _____! I
   PLURAL NOUN   NOUN

may be at the mall, and suddenly I'll jump into a fountain, do a/an

_____ jig, and splash _____ everywhere.
   ADJECTIVE   TYPE OF LIQUID

Or I could be grocery shopping with my mom and I'll suddenly

break into some impromptu tap _____, rhythmically
                          VERB ENDING IN "ING"

juggling canned _____ in the air. School is also a great
               PLURAL NOUN

place to show off my _____ moves. I love to slide down
                 ADJECTIVE

the hallway on my _____, then spring into the air and
             PART OF THE BODY

click my _____ together. I can't help myself. It
       PART OF THE BODY (PLURAL)

seems I was born to make (the) _____ a nicer place,
                          A PLACE

one _____ dance step at a time.
       ADJECTIVE

From DANCE MANIA MAD LIBS® • Copyright © 2009 by Penguin Random House LLC.

MAD LIBS® is fun to play with friends, but you can also play it by yourself! To begin with, DO NOT look at the story on the page below. Fill in the blanks on this page with the words called for. Then, using the words you have selected, fill in the blank spaces in the story.

Now you've created your own hilarious MAD LIBS® game!

BEHIND THE MASK

ADJECTIVE _____

NOUN _____

NOUN _____

NOUN _____

VERB ENDING IN "ING" _____

ADJECTIVE _____

PART OF THE BODY _____

ADJECTIVE _____

NOUN _____

ADJECTIVE _____

ADJECTIVE _____

ADJECTIVE _____

PART OF THE BODY (PLURAL) _____

NOUN _____

MAD LIBS®

BEHIND THE MASK

It's halftime, and your _____ moment is about
                              ADJECTIVE

to happen. You're waiting on the sidelines of the school

_____-ball field, and you're about to make your debut
    NOUN

as the school mascot: a polka-dotted _____ named
                                              NOUN

Captain _____-pants. Suddenly, the _____
         NOUN   VERB ENDING IN "ING"

band strikes up the music. They announce your _____
                                                    ADJECTIVE

name on the loudspeaker. You feel your heart beating in your

_____ as you run onto the center of the field and take
PART OF THE BODY

a/an _____ bow. You run from one end of the football
       ADJECTIVE

_____ to the other, performing your _____
    NOUN   ADJECTIVE

tricks in front of a stadium full of _____ fans. The crowd
                                          ADJECTIVE

loves you. The _____ cheerleaders run over and hoist
                    ADJECTIVE

you into the air on their _____. You feel like you're
                          PART OF THE BODY (PLURAL)

the _____ of the world!
        NOUN

From DANCE MANIA MAD LIBS® • Copyright © 2009 by Penguin Random House LLC.

MAD LIBS® is fun to play with friends, but you can also play it by yourself! To begin with, DO NOT look at the story on the page below. Fill in the blanks on this page with the words called for. Then, using the words you have selected, fill in the blank spaces in the story.

Now you've created your own hilarious MAD LIBS® game!

DANCING THROUGH THE DECADES

ADJECTIVE _____

ADJECTIVE _____

PLURAL NOUN _____

ARTICLE OF CLOTHING _____

PART OF THE BODY _____

ADJECTIVE _____

PART OF THE BODY (PLURAL) _____

NOUN _____

PLURAL NOUN _____

ADJECTIVE _____

PART OF THE BODY _____

PART OF THE BODY _____

ADJECTIVE _____

PLURAL NOUN _____

ADJECTIVE _____

ADJECTIVE _____

NOUN _____

ADJECTIVE _____

VERB _____

MAD LIBS®
DANCING THROUGH
THE DECADES

Dancing has always been a/an _____ pastime for the young
                ADJECTIVE

and _____. In the 1950s, _____ loved to go
     ADJECTIVE   PLURAL NOUN

to _____ hops and do the _____ jive.
  ARTICLE OF CLOTHING   PART OF THE BODY

In the '60s, it was The Twist—where you perform _____
                                     ADJECTIVE

dance moves while swinging your _____ from side
                       PART OF THE BODY (PLURAL)

to side. In the 1970s, dancers would disco under a glittery disco

_____ while wearing polyester _____. In
    NOUN   PLURAL NOUN

the '80s, it was truly _____ to break-dance—where you do
              ADJECTIVE

fancy _____-work and spin on your _____.
    PART OF THE BODY   PART OF THE BODY

In the _____ '90s, hip-hop and rap dominated the
     ADJECTIVE

music _____, and brought along with them a funky,
    PLURAL NOUN

_____ style of dance—not to mention the popular style
  ADJECTIVE

of wearing lots of _____ chains and rings. Although
              ADJECTIVE

dance crazes change with each decade, one _____
                                NOUN

remains the same: Dancing will always provide a/an _____
                                   ADJECTIVE

time if you just let loose and _____ to the music.
                      VERB

From DANCE MANIA MAD LIBS® • Copyright © 2009 by Penguin Random House LLC.

MAD LIBS® is fun to play with friends, but you can also play it by yourself! To begin with, DO NOT look at the story on the page below. Fill in the blanks on this page with the words called for. Then, using the words you have selected, fill in the blank spaces in the story.

Now you've created your own hilarious MAD LIBS® game!

RECITAL EXCITEMENT

PART OF THE BODY _____

PART OF THE BODY _____

ADJECTIVE _____

PLURAL NOUN _____

PLURAL NOUN _____

ADJECTIVE _____

PLURAL NOUN _____

ADJECTIVE _____

PLURAL NOUN _____

NOUN _____

ADJECTIVE _____

PLURAL NOUN _____

VERB (PAST TENSE) _____

ADJECTIVE _____

NOUN _____

ADJECTIVE _____

PLURAL NOUN _____

NOUN _____

MAD LIBS®

RECITAL EXCITEMENT

It's dance recital night, and you're so excited that you have a

lump in your _____ and your _____
    PART OF THE BODY   PART OF THE BODY

is beating wildly. You and your _____ dance class
                                      ADJECTIVE

are on pins and _____. While other dancers are putting
                PLURAL NOUN

_____ in their hair and dressing in _____
PLURAL NOUN   ADJECTIVE

costumes sparkling with sequins and tiny _____,
                                              PLURAL NOUN

you part the _____ curtains and sneak a peek at the
              ADJECTIVE

crowds of _____ filling the seats. Just before the
            PLURAL NOUN

_____ rises, your teacher says, "Go out there and make
    NOUN

your parents feel _____!" The overture begins—it's
                      ADJECTIVE

showtime! You and your fellow _____ dance like you've
                                  PLURAL NOUN

never _____ before. It's the most _____
        VERB (PAST TENSE)   ADJECTIVE

performance of your entire _____—and your
                                NOUN

_____ parents think so, too. After the show, they
    ADJECTIVE

give you a beautiful bouquet of _____. Their little
                                    PLURAL NOUN

_____ is a star!
    NOUN

From DANCE MANIA MAD LIBS® • Copyright © 2009 by Penguin Random House LLC.

MAD LIBS® is fun to play with friends, but you can also play it by yourself! To begin with, DO NOT look at the story on the page below. Fill in the blanks on this page with the words called for. Then, using the words you have selected, fill in the blank spaces in the story.

Now you've created your own hilarious MAD LIBS® game!

A NIGHT AT THE CARNIVAL

ADJECTIVE _____

PLURAL NOUN _____

NOUN _____

ADJECTIVE _____

NUMBER _____

PART OF THE BODY (PLURAL) _____

PART OF THE BODY (PLURAL) _____

ADJECTIVE _____

PLURAL NOUN _____

PLURAL NOUN _____

VERB ENDING IN "ING" _____

NOUN _____

VERB ENDING IN "ING" _____

PART OF THE BODY (PLURAL) _____

PLURAL NOUN _____

NOUN _____

ADJECTIVE _____

PLURAL NOUN _____

MAD LIBS®

A NIGHT AT THE CARNIVAL

When my best friend and I go to the carnival, we go on as

many _____ rides as we can before we run out of
　　　　　ADJECTIVE

_____. Our first must is the roller-_____.
　PLURAL NOUN　　　　　　　　　　　　　　　　　　　NOUN

What a/an _____ thrill—racing down the track at
　　　　　　ADJECTIVE

_____ miles an hour, throwing our _____
　NUMBER　　　　　　　　　　　　　　　PART OF THE BODY (PLURAL)

into the air, and screaming at the top of our _____.
　　　　　　　　　　　　　　　　　　　　　PART OF THE BODY (PLURAL)

Not as terrifying—but still _____ fun—are the
　　　　　　　　　　　　　ADJECTIVE

bumper _____, where we drive around like crazy
　　　　PLURAL NOUN

_____ _____ into each other.
　PLURAL NOUN　　　VERB ENDING IN "ING"

By far the scariest ride is the Tilt-a/an-_____. It
　　　　　　　　　　　　　　　　　　　　　NOUN

sends us _____ in circles so fast it makes
　　　　VERB ENDING IN "ING"

our _____ spin. After that, we're happy as
　　PART OF THE BODY (PLURAL)

_____ to hop on the Ferris _____ and
　PLURAL NOUN　　　　　　　　　　　　　　　NOUN

enjoy the slow _____ ride. It's a nice way to top off the
　　　　　　　ADJECTIVE

evening and calm our _____.
　　　　　　　　　　PLURAL NOUN

From DANCE MANIA MAD LIBS® • Copyright © 2009 by Penguin Random House LLC.

MAD LIBS® is fun to play with friends, but you can also play it by yourself! To begin with, DO NOT look at the story on the page below. Fill in the blanks on this page with the words called for. Then, using the words you have selected, fill in the blank spaces in the story.

Now you've created your own hilarious MAD LIBS® game!

FANCY PANTS
DANCE SCHOOL

ADVERB _____

PERSON IN ROOM (FEMALE) _____

A PLACE _____

ADJECTIVE _____

ADJECTIVE _____

ADJECTIVE _____

ADJECTIVE _____

ADJECTIVE _____

PART OF THE BODY (PLURAL) _____

ADJECTIVE _____

PLURAL NOUN _____

PLURAL NOUN _____

ADJECTIVE _____

PART OF THE BODY (PLURAL) _____

VERB ENDING IN "ING" _____

PART OF THE BODY (PLURAL) _____

NOUN _____

ADJECTIVE _____

MAD LIBS®
FANCY PANTS
DANCE SCHOOL

We would like to _____ inform you that you have been
                       ADVERB

accepted by Madame _____'s Dance School, the
                    PERSON IN ROOM (FEMALE)

premier dance school in (the) _____. Here is a list of
                               A PLACE

the _____ courses we offer:
     ADJECTIVE

- **Ballet:** A/An _____ form of dance with its
                   ADJECTIVE

  _____ origins in the French court. You'll learn to
   ADJECTIVE

  perform with _____ grace and _____
                ADJECTIVE   ADJECTIVE

  elegance while twirling on the tips of your _____.
                                              PART OF THE BODY (PLURAL)

- **Tap:** The name comes from the _____ sound made
                                   ADJECTIVE

  when metal _____ on the dancer's _____
             PLURAL NOUN   PLURAL NOUN

  touch a/an _____ surface. We'll teach you to rhythmically
             ADJECTIVE

  tap your _____.
           PART OF THE BODY (PLURAL)

- **Irish Step** _____: You will learn to be swift on your
                 VERB ENDING IN "ING"

  _____ and stand straight as a/an _____
   PART OF THE BODY (PLURAL)   NOUN

  as you perform _____ Irish folk dances.
                 ADJECTIVE

From DANCE MANIA MAD LIBS® • Copyright © 2009 by Penguin Random House LLC.

MAD LIBS® is fun to play with friends, but you can also play it by yourself! To begin with, DO NOT look at the story on the page below. Fill in the blanks on this page with the words called for. Then, using the words you have selected, fill in the blank spaces in the story.

Now you've created your own hilarious MAD LIBS® game!

ALL THE RIGHT MOVES

NUMBER _____

ADJECTIVE _____

ADJECTIVE _____

PERSON IN ROOM _____

ADJECTIVE _____

TYPE OF LIQUID _____

PART OF THE BODY _____

NOUN _____

ADJECTIVE _____

ADJECTIVE _____

PLURAL NOUN _____

ADVERB _____

NOUN _____

MAD LIBS

ALL THE RIGHT MOVES

It's been _____ grueling weeks on *Gotta Dance,*
　　　　　　NUMBER

America's latest and greatest _____ reality show. Now
　　　　　　　　　　　　　　ADJECTIVE

it's down to just two _____ dancers—you and the
　　　　　　　　　　　ADJECTIVE

crowd favorite, _____. Tonight, the _____
　　　　　PERSON IN ROOM　　　　　　　　　ADJECTIVE

winner will be crowned. Understandably, you're nervous. Beads

of _____ drip down your _____ as you
　　TYPE OF LIQUID　　　　　　　　　PART OF THE BODY

wait to begin your final _____. The music starts and
　　　　　　　　　　　　NOUN

you perform a dramatic series of _____ leaps, twirls,
　　　　　　　　　　　　　　ADJECTIVE

and twists, topping it with a/an _____ finish that has
　　　　　　　　　　　　　ADJECTIVE

the judges leaping to their _____ and applauding
　　　　　　　　　　PLURAL NOUN

_____. You've got the win in the bag—and if anyone
ADVERB

deserves to be in the _____-light, it's you!
　　　　　　　　　NOUN

From DANCE MANIA MAD LIBS® • Copyright © 2009 by Penguin Random House LLC.

MAD LIBS® is fun to play with friends, but you can also play it by yourself! To begin with, DO NOT look at the story on the page below. Fill in the blanks on this page with the words called for. Then, using the words you have selected, fill in the blank spaces in the story.

Now you've created your own hilarious MAD LIBS® game!

EXTREME MAKEOVER: BEDROOM EDITION

NOUN _____

ADJECTIVE _____

PLURAL NOUN _____

ADVERB _____

ADJECTIVE _____

PLURAL NOUN _____

NOUN _____

ADJECTIVE _____

COLOR _____

PLURAL NOUN _____

ADJECTIVE _____

PLURAL NOUN _____

ADJECTIVE _____

ADJECTIVE _____

CELEBRITY (MALE) _____

VERB _____

ADJECTIVE _____

I won a contest in *Teen* _____ magazine! The prize?
                           NOUN

A/An _____ bedroom makeover with all the bells
       ADJECTIVE

and _____, to be _____ displayed
        PLURAL NOUN   ADVERB

in an upcoming issue. Since I'm a/an _____ princess
                                        ADJECTIVE

at heart, I picked a royal theme. Ribbons and ruffles and

_____—oh my! First, I painted my _____
  PLURAL NOUN   NOUN

a/an _____ shade of royal _____. Then
       ADJECTIVE   COLOR

I decorated my walls with jeweled _____. Next I
                                      PLURAL NOUN

added a/an _____ bedspread covered in frilly
               ADJECTIVE

_____. I even got a/an _____ throne to sit
  PLURAL NOUN   ADJECTIVE

on! Finally, I hung up a wall-sized poster of my _____
                                                    ADJECTIVE

heartthrob, _____. As long as I'm going to
               CELEBRITY (MALE)

_____ in a room befitting a princess, I might as well
   VERB

have a/an _____ prince by my side!
              ADJECTIVE

From DANCE MANIA MAD LIBS® • Copyright © 2009 by Penguin Random House LLC.

MAD LIBS® is fun to play with friends, but you can also play it by yourself! To begin with, DO NOT look at the story on the page below. Fill in the blanks on this page with the words called for. Then, using the words you have selected, fill in the blank spaces in the story.

Now you've created your own hilarious MAD LIBS® game!

I DO, I DANCE

ADJECTIVE _____

ADVERB _____

NOUN _____

NOUN _____

NOUN _____

PART OF THE BODY (PLURAL) _____

ADJECTIVE _____

ADJECTIVE _____

PART OF THE BODY (PLURAL) _____

PART OF THE BODY (PLURAL) _____

A PLACE _____

PART OF THE BODY _____

SAME PART OF THE BODY _____

SAME PART OF THE BODY _____

VERB _____

NOUN _____

ADJECTIVE _____

NOUN _____

MAD LIBS

I DO, I DANCE

You're sure to find _____ dancing at wedding receptions.

ADJECTIVE

There's something very special and _____ touching when

ADVERB

the bride and _____ have their first dance as husband

NOUN

and _____. And doesn't the father-_____ dance

NOUN NOUN

always bring tears to your _____? But when the

PART OF THE BODY (PLURAL)

DJ starts playing _____ wedding classics, that's when

ADJECTIVE

the _____ fun begins. Who doesn't love the Chicken

ADJECTIVE

Dance, where you poke out your _____ and flap

PART OF THE BODY (PLURAL)

them around? Or there's the conga line, where you grab someone

by the _____, fall in line, and snake around (the)

PART OF THE BODY (PLURAL)

_____. The Hokey Pokey is great, too: You put your right

A PLACE

_____ in, you put your right _____ out,

PART OF THE BODY SAME PART OF THE BODY

you put your right _____ in, and you _____

SAME PART OF THE BODY VERB

it all about. Yep, wedding receptions are where it's at—just don't get

so caught up shaking your groove-_____ that you forget to

NOUN

eat a/an _____ piece of wedding _____!

ADJECTIVE NOUN

From DANCE MANIA MAD LIBS® • Copyright © 2009 by Penguin Random House LLC.

MAD LIBS® is fun to play with friends, but you can also play it by yourself! To begin with, DO NOT look at the story on the page below. Fill in the blanks on this page with the words called for. Then, using the words you have selected, fill in the blank spaces in the story.

Now you've created your own hilarious MAD LIBS® game!

A CLASS ACT

NOUN _____

PART OF THE BODY _____

PLURAL NOUN _____

ADJECTIVE _____

ADVERB _____

PERSON IN ROOM _____

NOUN _____

PLURAL NOUN _____

PERSON IN ROOM _____

ADJECTIVE _____

CELEBRITY_____

PERSON IN ROOM (FEMALE) _____

PART OF THE BODY _____

ADJECTIVE _____

ADJECTIVE _____

VERB ENDING IN "ING" _____

PART OF THE BODY (PLURAL) _____

ADJECTIVE _____

NOUN _____

PLURAL NOUN _____

MAD LIBS

A CLASS ACT

I've always wanted to enter the school talent _____,

NOUN

but the thought of being on stage makes my _____

PART OF THE BODY

tremble with fear. This year, I decided to face my _____,

PLURAL NOUN

and I entered the _____ contest. The competition was

ADJECTIVE

_____ fierce. _____ rode a/an _____

ADVERB · PERSON IN ROOM · NOUN

while juggling _____. _____ did

PLURAL NOUN · PERSON IN ROOM

a/an _____ impersonation of _____. And

ADJECTIVE · CELEBRITY

_____ sang her _____ out with a/an

PERSON IN ROOM (FEMALE) · PART OF THE BODY

_____ rendition of "_____ Days Are Here Again."

ADJECTIVE · ADJECTIVE

Finally, it was my turn. I did a dance routine that had the audience

_____ in their seats. Afterward, I closed my eyes and

VERB ENDING IN "ING"

crossed my _____ for good luck. Suddenly I heard

PART OF THE BODY (PLURAL)

the principal say, "And this year's _____ winner is ..."—

ADJECTIVE

and it was me! When he handed me the _____-shaped

NOUN

trophy, I held it up triumphantly and said, "This is for all the little

_____ that helped me along the way!"

PLURAL NOUN

From DANCE MANIA MAD LIBS® • Copyright © 2009 by Penguin Random House LLC.

MAD LIBS® is fun to play with friends, but you can also play it by yourself! To begin with, DO NOT look at the story on the page below. Fill in the blanks on this page with the words called for. Then, using the words you have selected, fill in the blank spaces in the story.

Now you've created your own hilarious MAD LIBS® game!

WALKING THE RED CARPET

PLURAL NOUN _____

NOUN _____

ADVERB _____

NOUN _____

ARTICLE OF CLOTHING (PLURAL) _____

ADJECTIVE _____

NOUN _____

ADJECTIVE _____

CELEBRITY (MALE) _____

NOUN _____

NOUN _____

ADJECTIVE _____

VERB (PAST TENSE) _____

ADJECTIVE _____

PLURAL NOUN _____

PART OF THE BODY (PLURAL) _____

ADJECTIVE _____

PART OF THE BODY (PLURAL) _____

MAD LIBS

WALKING THE RED CARPET

I entered a sweepstakes and won four _____ to a/an
                                        PLURAL NOUN

_____-studded movie premiere! The big night arrived,
   NOUN

and my friends and I waited _____ until a black
                                   ADVERB

stretch _____ pulled into my driveway. We were all
            NOUN

dressed in fancy _____—and boy, did we
                     ARTICLE OF CLOTHING (PLURAL)

look _____! When we got to the theater, we strutted
        ADJECTIVE

down the red _____ like we were _____
                  NOUN   ADJECTIVE

celebrities. We even saw the movie's star, _____—the
                                              CELEBRITY (MALE)

love of my _____! But before I could get him to
                 NOUN

sign my _____, we had to go inside and watch the
            NOUN

_____ movie. We laughed, we cried, we _____.
   ADJECTIVE   VERB (PAST TENSE)

When the premiere was over and we were headed home in the

_____ limo, we turned the music up, sang at the top of
   ADJECTIVE

our _____, and stuck our _____ out of
       PLURAL NOUN   PART OF THE BODY (PLURAL)

the sunroof. It was a blast! Like the movie, this _____
                                                       ADJECTIVE

night earned two _____ up.
                    PART OF THE BODY (PLURAL)

From DANCE MANIA MAD LIBS® • Copyright © 2009 by Penguin Random House LLC.

MAD LIBS® is fun to play with friends, but you can also play it by yourself! To begin with, DO NOT look at the story on the page below. Fill in the blanks on this page with the words called for. Then, using the words you have selected, fill in the blank spaces in the story.

Now you've created your own hilarious MAD LIBS® game!

COOL MOVES

VERB ENDING IN "ING" _____

PERSON IN ROOM (MALE) _____

PERSON IN ROOM (FEMALE) _____

ADJECTIVE _____

ADJECTIVE _____

EXCLAMATION _____

PART OF THE BODY _____

ADJECTIVE _____

VERB ENDING IN "ING" _____

PLURAL NOUN _____

ADJECTIVE _____

ADJECTIVE _____

NUMBER _____

NOUN _____

PLURAL NOUN _____

NOUN _____

PLURAL NOUN _____

A PLACE _____

MA○L○T
COOL MOVES

It's the World Ice _____ Championships, and
                        VERB ENDING IN "ING"

_____ and _____ are hoping to
  PERSON IN ROOM (MALE)   PERSON IN ROOM (FEMALE)

win a/an _____ medal! Let's listen to the commentary as
            ADJECTIVE

this _____ duo finishes their routine.
        ADJECTIVE

Announcer #1: _____! He's holding her in the air by her
                    EXCLAMATION

_____—a/an _____ lift no other pair can do.
  PART OF THE BODY   ADJECTIVE

Announcer #2: And now, in these few final seconds, they're

_____ across the ice like a pair of _____.
    VERB ENDING IN "ING"   PLURAL NOUN

It's a/an _____ finish to their _____ performance.
             ADJECTIVE   ADJECTIVE

Announcer #1: Look—a perfect _____ from the judges!
                                    NUMBER

They did it!

Announcer #2: The _____ is going wild, littering the ice
                        NOUN

with _____. This performance proved beyond a shadow
      PLURAL NOUN

of a/an _____ that this pair of _____ is the best
           NOUN   PLURAL NOUN

in (the) _____!
          A PLACE

From DANCE MANIA MAD LIBS® • Copyright © 2009 by Penguin Random House LLC.

MAD LIBS® is fun to play with friends, but you can also play it by yourself! To begin with, DO NOT look at the story on the page below. Fill in the blanks on this page with the words called for. Then, using the words you have selected, fill in the blank spaces in the story.

Now you've created your own hilarious MAD LIBS® game!

DANCE TILL YOU DROP

ADJECTIVE _____

ADJECTIVE _____

NOUN _____

NUMBER _____

PERSON IN ROOM _____

NOUN _____

VERB ENDING IN "ING" _____

NOUN _____

ADVERB _____

ANIMAL (PLURAL) _____

ADJECTIVE _____

PLURAL NOUN _____

VERB _____

NOUN _____

PART OF THE BODY _____

NOUN _____

PLURAL NOUN _____

PLURAL NOUN _____

MAD LIBS

DANCE TILL YOU DROP

Today's the day: It's "The Last Chance to Dance," a/an _____
ADJECTIVE

school dance-a-thon to raise money for a/an _____ cause.
ADJECTIVE

The goal: to be the last _____ dancing. You've collected
NOUN

more than _____ dollars in pledges from your parents,
NUMBER

your best friend, _____, and even your reluctant
PERSON IN ROOM

next-door _____. You've spent hours _____
NOUN VERB ENDING IN "ING"

to build up your stamina. So you're totally ready when the

_____-a-thon begins. The hours pass by _____,
NOUN ADVERB

and other dancers are dropping like _____. You're starting
ANIMAL (PLURAL)

to feel a little _____, too. But finally, it's down to just two
ADJECTIVE

_____—including you. Just when you think you can't
PLURAL NOUN

_____ for one more second, the other _____
VERB NOUN

collapses into a chair. The emcee grabs your _____,
PART OF THE BODY

lifts it high in the air, and declares you the _____! And
NOUN

even though your legs are as wobbly as rubber _____,
PLURAL NOUN

you feel like a million _____!
PLURAL NOUN

From DANCE MANIA MAD LIBS® • Copyright © 2009 by Penguin Random House LLC.

MAD LIBS® is fun to play with friends, but you can also play it by yourself! To begin with, DO NOT look at the story on the page below. Fill in the blanks on this page with the words called for. Then, using the words you have selected, fill in the blank spaces in the story.

Now you've created your own hilarious MAD LIBS® game!

STREET BEAT

ADJECTIVE _____

NOUN _____

VERB _____

PERSON IN ROOM _____

PERSON IN ROOM _____

ADJECTIVE _____

ADJECTIVE _____

A PLACE _____

ADJECTIVE _____

NOUN _____

NOUN _____

PART OF THE BODY (PLURAL) _____

ADJECTIVE _____

VERB _____

PLURAL NOUN _____

PLURAL NOUN _____

ADJECTIVE _____

ADVERB _____

PART OF THE BODY _____

STREET BEAT

Whenever people walk past the corner of _____
ADJECTIVE

Avenue and _____ Street, they immediately stop
NOUN

and _____: It's Lil' _____ and YoYo
VERB   PERSON IN ROOM

_____ performing their _____ street
PERSON IN ROOM   ADJECTIVE

music. This _____ duo is famous throughout (the)
ADJECTIVE

_____ for their _____ orchestra of street
A PLACE   ADJECTIVE

sounds. They clang the lids from _____ cans. They
NOUN

bounce _____-balls on the ground while stomping their
NOUN

_____. They use brooms to make _____
PART OF THE BODY (PLURAL)   ADJECTIVE

sweeping sounds on the sidewalk and they use the handles to

_____ rhythmically against _____ parked on
VERB   PLURAL NOUN

the street. They're having the time of their _____—and the
PLURAL NOUN

same goes for the _____ onlookers who _____
ADJECTIVE   ADVERB

clap their _____ at the end of each and every number.
PART OF THE BODY

From DANCE MANIA MAD LIBS® • Copyright © 2009 by Penguin Random House LLC.

Download Mad Libs today!

Join the millions of Mad Libs fans
creating wacky and wonderful
stories on our apps!